Through THE EYES OF A CHILD

Lila Jane Tibbitts

Outskirts Press, Inc.
Denver, Colorado

Outskirts Press, Inc.
http://www.outskirtspress.com

ISBN: 978-1-4327-1881-7

Outskirts Press and the "OP" logo are trademarks belonging to Outskirts Press, Inc.

INTRODUCTION

As I began to write this book it was a matter of remembering the wonderful times I had personally as a child. I shared this information with my family, and we laughed hysterically over some of the incidents, and I do pray that some of you can go back in time with me and remember some of your wonderful childhood moments as well.

Things suddenly became serious as I realized how our times have changed, some in good ways, others in very negative ways.

Do you remember when you first started school? Do you remember how we started our classes? Do you remember standing with our hands over our hearts and pledging allegiance to the flag of the United States? Do you remember everybody saying "The Lord's Prayer?" Sometimes we even sang, "God Bless America." In our school we had a short Bible reading from the Old and New Testaments, and nobody complained; we had Protestants, Catholics, Jewish, and Native American children in our school system.

What happened to the freedoms that were fought for? What happened to the integrity of our country and its leaders?

Yes, folks, things have changed! We have a very low percentage of people who are dissatisfied with prayer and the Word of God being displayed and spoken anywhere in the United States; and yes, they have a right to their opinions and belief systems if they have any at all, but what I am trying to figure out is this: Why should 12% of the population make laws for the other 88% of us? Why should our Supreme Court bow to the 12%?

We have trouble in our school systems from grade school on up; we have bullying, murders and guns in our schools, and some of the students find it so interesting they video all of the action and spread it around on the Internet. It seems we have gone back to the arenas, where it was man against the wild beasts...but who have become the bloodthirsty wild beasts now?

Our country was founded on Bible-believing men of God. Yes, they had frailties like all of us and were not perfect...but they sought the counsel of God when creating the Declaration of Independence, and the Constitution of the United States, and in making important decisions like the freeing of slaves.

I happened to grow up in New England, where there were very few African Americans. We did have Native Americans, and we all got along; at least I thought we did, until one day I heard my grandfather talking about a family that he called "half-breeds." I thought to myself, that doesn't sound very kind, so I asked him what he was talking about. He began to rant and rave about black people coming to Maine and breeding with Indians, who were also not on his favored list.

I remember asking him why he hated these people without provocation, and he had no real answer. I realized even as a child no law can legislate love and kindness, and the difficult thing for me to understand is this: it still continues. Why do some people apparently need somebody else to look down upon? God made different skin-colored people; He made different shaped eyes and hair of various colors. Why can't we just accept each other as God made us, instead of differentiating when we speak of friends from other cultures?

When our youngest daughter was in elementary school in Maryland, we had a teacher's conference, and although she talked a great deal about her teacher, we didn't know until we met her she was African American, and I signify that as a compliment to our daughter. You see, to children race doesn't matter, IF they haven't been told derogatory things about race from their family or friends.

We have taken prayer and Bible reading out of our schools and have replaced them with witchcraft, Zen, yoga, and just about anything EXCEPT Bible clubs or Bible studies, which are not allowed. We now have stabbings and oral sex on buses and shootings on school and university campuses. What is going on? We had never heard of such things when I was a child. How scary it must be for children to have to ride a school bus today! We walked to school if we were within a mile of the schools; it was good for us. Yes, there were a few bullies we contended with, but not to the extent of things today.

Our world has changed; both parents have to work just to pay the bills and keep the family clothed, fed, and educated, whereas, my mom was home waiting for us with a nice snack prepared, excited to hear about our day. We, all of us, have got to get back to the basics of life. We need the Lord in our lives; we need to re-establish the family altar; we need to listen to our children, teach them to make the right choices, and encourage them to be all that they can be in Jesus Christ.

Now on the lighter side of life, I would like to share with you some of my precious memories, and prayerfully, they will put a smile on your face and stir up good memories in your heart.

DEDICATION

It is with great pleasure that I dedicate this book to my Lord and Savior, Jesus Christ, who, having the greatest sense of humor, created us.

To my husband and best friend, Frank, and to my children, Lisa Jayne, Jeffrey Owen, and Loren Irene; may they have as much fun growing with their children and grandchildren as I have experienced.

I thank God for giving me such a rich childhood with parents Owen and Arlene Wardwell, brother Doug, and sister Judith Ann as well as grand-parents who loved me and showed their love consistently.

I thank the Lord for the talents that He bestowed upon our family; the music we have enjoyed as well as the ability to write music the Lord has given to Frank and me to share with the world.

Philippians 1:3

"I thank my God upon every remembrance of you."

FOREWORD

This book is written to share with you some of the comical things that truly happened in my childhood.

It also shows some of the inconsistencies in the Christian Walk many of us have experienced and continue to experience. It typifies the personal relationship that the Lord Jesus Christ desires us to have with Him on every level of life. His desire is that we walk with Him daily, seeing that He enjoys our company, as well as our appreciation of him in our daily walk.

These are actual happenings in my life, and there are many more that will be shared in a forthcoming book. I pray that this book brings back some of your own fond memories of childhood and puts a smile on your face.

Feel free to share with me some of your funny experiences, so we can laugh together over our humanity.

May the Lord help us to not take ourselves too seriously!

I am telling these stories as a child of nine years old would relate them, perhaps because I remember exactly as it was when I was a child, and perhaps I don't want to grow up anymore.

TABLE OF CONTENTS

ROLL OUT THE BARRELS

Well, Lord, thanks for making today such a fun-filled day, especially since I had to stay in my own yard four whole hours…but you were right there with me, so it wasn't so bad. Ya know what? I think if I sit real quiet, that beautiful robin will come right to me and eat the bread right out of my hand. Whaddaya think, Lord?

Today was a funny day. It rained in the afternoon as you know, 'cause the flowers have to grow. We were all playing in our garage that we share with the principal of the school, just having a great time. They had five big ol' pickle barrels on their side of the garage all lined up, so we jumped on 'em, makin' lots of noise when they knocked together, and started singin' "Roll Out the Barrel," when the principal's wife came out and screamed at us at the top of her lungs. Her mouth was open wide, and just then a seagull flew over and went number two right in her mouth. We tried real hard not to laugh, but we couldn't help it, Lord. I do hope you'll forgive me.

That lady grabbed me some fast, she did; almost ripped my sweater. She dragged me to my house and told my mother what a terrible child I was 'cause I laughed right out loud at what happened. She told my mother I needed a real bad spanking and to keep me out of her side of the garage. My mother started to giggle; she tried hard not to, but it slipped right out. That woman slammed our door so hard she cracked the glass in our door, but Mom and I just laughed and laughed and laughed. When Daddy came home, he laughed until tears ran out of his eyes, and I didn't get a spanking. Tell me, Lord, did you laugh too?

IT'S SHOWTIME

First of all, Lord, I'd like to thank you for making mornings so beautiful. When I look at the sun shining, it's like you're saying just to me, "C'mon, what's keepin' you? Let's have some fun!"

I ran up to my friends' house, Peta and Patty, the twins; they leave the back door open for me so I won't wake the rest of the family up. I really do like to wake the twins up, 'cause then we plan out the whole day for the neighborhood.

Today we decided to put on a "Gay Nineties Show" just like the grown-ups did last week. Now I don't know whether it is 1890 or 1899 or what or even why they call it that…but anyway, we did the planning. We called all the kids together and ev'rything, and we gave out all the parts, and guess what I am. Well, you already know, a bird in a jilted cage, or sump'n' like that. Peta is the man on the flyin' trapeze. She's chubby like me, and she fell off and hurt herself, but went up and tried it again anyway. She made it on the third try, and everybody clapped and stuff.

Patty was the vamp from Sabanna, wherever that is! Mom says Patty is pateet; she's kinda skinny and doesn't like to get dirty like Peta and me. We dressed her up with lipstick and the red stuff moms put on their cheeks, even red finganail polish. She danced around just like the woman did in the show last week, just a swingin' this piece of cloth we taped seagull feathers to, and she was quite a hit. We invited the whole neighborhood. We even let some of the boys take part, and everybody thought it was real good. All of our parents came, and we made them pay five cents to watch it. Did you like it, Lord?

I'm a little sad though, 'cause after the show Peta and Patty's mother told me I couldn't go to their house until after nine o'clock. Boy, oh boy! Half the day's gone by then, Lord! Now whaddaya think of that?

Well, guess that's all for me tonight, Lord, I sure am glad you like to get up early, Lord. I love you more than anybody else in the whole world. Tell me, Lord, why don't parents like to get up in the morning?

MAKIN' HOMEMADE WINE

This was a very strange day, but it was a beautiful day. The robin came up to my chair today; he was cockin' his little head at me, but I made the mistake of reaching out to him, and he flew away. I hope you'll tell him to come back tomorrow, Lord, please! My Sunday school teacher says you can make anything happen that you want, but you'll only do what is good for you and me.

It must be hard makin' all those decisions every day; I pray you'll have lots of strength! That's what Mom says all the time. She does sump'n' funny with her teeth and mouth when she says, "God, give me strength." All I can see is her funny mouth and teeth when she says it, but I can still hear it.

My friend Helen and I went pickin' grapes. Now we live in Claremont, New Hampshire, but we were pickin' Concord grapes. I can't figure that one out, Lord, but we got'em anyway. You know, those grapes are big and purple and taste good, and we remembered that you made wine in the Bible, so we decided to do that too.

My friend's father owns a gas station and has lots of paper cups in the toilet, so we got a whole bunch of 'em and decided we would squeeze the grapes and sell it for five cents a cup. Nobody ever told us what wine was, so we asked Mom, who knows just about everything. She said, "People put the grapes in a big tub, and they smash them with their feet," so we decided to try it.

It was awful hot that day, and we were really sweaty and thirsty; so was everybody else, so we knew we could make lots of money sellin' our smashed grape wine! We took our shoes and socks off, put all the grapes in Mom's big old washtub, and squished grapes. Our feet turned purple, our clothes turned purple, and we were purple from head to foot. We tried drinkin' some. It was awful lumpy, but it tasted pretty good. We sold all we had to the kids...but then guess who came by all huffy and puffy? The principal's wife! She went and told my mother, and Mom came out screaming. Her face got all red, and when she gets mad, she talks through her teeth so I can hardly understand a word she says, but I know I'm in trouble when she starts talkin' that way. Do you talk through your teeth, Lord?

Mom soaked me for two hours in the tub, but I'm still purple. Tell me, Jesus, was that a sin?

FUN AT THE LAKE!

Tell me, Lord, do you like to go fishin'? I went down and fished off the bridge today, and guess what, I caught the biggest pickerel that's come out of the lake. That's what the old man said, and he fishes there every day. He told me I would never catch anything with the hook I had, but right after I put my line in, I caught the biggest fish I've ever seen. It almost pulled me off the bridge, but I hung on for dear life. I brought it up to Daddy, and he couldn't believe his eyes. I sure am thankful that you made this lake, it is beautiful, and I hope nobody catches any bigger fish than mine. Thanks for letting me catch it, Lord.

Every day is exciting here at camp, Lord! This afternoon Dougie, my brother, and I went out playing around in the boat. We washed it all out and got it ready to go fishin' later on, so we decided to clean ourselves off before Mom yelled at us for bein' dirty, and all of a sudden, Dougie jumps up and down in the water and pulls his swimmin' trunks down. I closed my eyes real quick, 'cause now that we're older we're not supposed to see each other's private parts. Dougie had five toads in his trunks. Can you believe that? He sure did look funny jumpin' up and down tryin' to get them out; probably scared them half to death!

We wash our hair in the lake with Ivory soap; do you ever do that, Lord? We were all down by the shore lyin' on the big rocks, and when I stood up my foot hit the soap, and I slipped and fell into some other big rocks and hurt my foot really bad, and my mother stood over me and laughed and laughed! You know, Lord, I coulda killed myself; thanks for not letting me get hurt any worse than I was. Daddy didn't laugh; he picked me up and held me. I was almost tempted to talk through my teeth. Maybe it's catchin' Lord!

THE NEIGHBORHOOD BULLY

T oday was a really special day, Lord! Thank you for sending the robin back to me again, 'cause he ate right out of my hand.

Today was the day we caught us a bully! I don't know why he likes to tease everybody. My sister has brain damage, and he teases her and sneaks up on her and makes her fall down on purpose; now you know that's not a nice thing to do, Lord. The bully's name is David, and he has killed two cats and one dog and stomped through everybody's gardens. All of us kids got together and decided to teach him a lesson. My big brother even got in on it; so did some of the other kids' older brothers and sisters.

Here's what happened: my sister was playing in our back yard by the swing set, and David climbed over the fence and waited until Judy got in front of the swing and pushed the swing hard so it hit her in the head. My sister cried and cried, and my mom came out and scolded David. She told him she was going to talk to his father when he got home.

We decided to spy on David. We even set a trap right where he climbs over the fence. We were all skulkin' around hiding behind houses and trees, and Judy was out playing again, and we saw David try to sneak up on her, but I jumped right out, and I dared him to touch her. Well, Lord, he came at me with a hatchet and said he was gonna cut my pigtails right off! I scratched and kicked him and then all the other kids came out and piled right on top of him and beat him up. For the first time we know of, David went home crying, and we all felt really good about it. Was that a sin?

His mother is real nice. She's had a breakup of nerves or sump'n' like that; anyway, everybody says she's crazy, but she's not. She paints her toes and finganails red, and she talks to me sometimes, and she told me she likes me a lot, 'cause I'm the only one who will sit and talk with her. David's father gets awful mad when he sees her talking with me and tells her to get in the house. She told me if she doesn't do what he tells her to do, he will beat her up. Mom and Daddy don't do that. I don't think that's right, do you, Lord?

Anyway, when Daddy got home and found out all that had happened that day, he got ready to go over and talk to David's father, but just as he was leaving, here comes David's father with the hatchet in his hand. I sure prayed hard that you'd make David's father miss if he tried to hit Daddy! Daddy tried to talk to him, but all he kept saying was, "They were being poisecuted," whatever that means. Is that like the electric chair? Then he threw the hatchet, and the back of it hit my mother's foot.

Boy, oh boy, Mom called on you for help again, and then she started talkin' through her teeth again, and Daddy started over the fence after David's father. David's father ran and locked himself in the house and wouldn't come out.

I told Mom and Daddy that you told us to forgive our enemies, but they were both talkin' through their teeth. Talkin' through your teeth must be catchin', huh, Lord?

AUNT ALICE'S PIE

We went out to visit Grammy and Papa today, Lord, and boy did I get into trouble! I love to visit them in Meddybemps. They really love us lots and let us do almost anything we want to do except when Mom and Daddy are there.

Aunt Alice was there just a cookin' away; she makes lovely pies and stuff. When it's dinnertime we all sit down around this great big oak table and its lots of fun with everybody talkin' at once. Daddy says, "You can't hear yourself think." Well, Lord, I didn't think thoughts made a sound, but maybe they do.

The dinner was really good...until dessert. I took one taste of my pie, and it was terrible. I refused to eat it, and Mom and Daddy were glaring at me and Mom was talking through her teeth at me, and then Aunt Alice got big tears in her big brown eyes, and I got sent away from the table. I can't eat things that don't taste good to me, Lord; would you? Pretty soon after everybody finished eating, I heard people getting sick, and guess what? Everybody but me got sick, and I was the only one who didn't eat the pie. They discovered that Aunt Alice had used wallpaper paste instead of flour to make her pies. Lord, couldn't you have stopped her from doing that? Anyway, they all told me they were sorry they punished me. Sometimes parents should listen to the kids, huh, Lord?

IT'S WINTER!

Today was not such a good day, Lord; it is not fun to stay in my bedroom until everybody else gets up. I looked out my window and saw just a few birds around, but there was lots and lots of snow. I love snow, Lord. I could hardly wait to go outside and slide down the hill. Everybody heard me open my door, and they all stuck their heads out of their bedrooms doors and yelled at me. I don't think that's a very nice way to say good morning, do you? Today is Saturday, too!

Daddy was the next one up, and we had a good time cookin' breakfast together. Daddy always sings at the top of his voice, "O Sole Amio," whatever that is, but it gets Mom up faster, anyway. Mom is actin' kinda strange today; she's talkin' through her teeth again.

I'm so big now I can dress myself, but my sister has to have lots of help, and I kinda have to take care of her when we go outside to play. In the summer it's not so bad, but in the winter it is terrible. Mom gets Judy into so many snow pants and sweaters and things she can hardly walk or bend her knees. Mom gets Judy all ready, and in just a few minutes, Judy has to go to the toilet. This goes on about ten million times. I get tired of bringin' her in and takin' her out and Mom gets tired of dressing and undressing her.

Everybody knows you're not supposed to wet your pants, but Mom said if she comes in again she'd have to stay in and so would I, 'cause she had important things to do that day. About ten minutes went by, and Judy started pulling at me. I told her to just wet herself and stay out, so she did! I was sliding with my friends, and when I looked for Judy, there she was, standing up in a real funny position. I called to her, but she didn't move. I ran up to her, and guess what, Lord, she was frozen and couldn't make her legs move. My friends and I laid her on a sled and pulled her home. Was Mom ever mad! She asked you for strength again with her teeth showing. I didn't know that pee would freeze. Did you, Lord?

I know I was to blame for Judy wetting herself and Mom talking through her teeth again, but Judy came over and sat in my lap. She wasn't angry at me at all, but Mom was still talking through her teeth.

MY BIG BROTHER

This morning was really wonderful, Lord! My big brother, Dougie, got up real early and got dressed in his hiking clothes and said <u>IF</u> I could get ready in three minutes, I could go. It took him twenty minutes to get ready. He looked kinda disappointed when I came out, but boy, oh boy did I have fun.

Dougie knows as much as you do about the woods; he told me so! We went up two mountains, one big one and one little one. When we got to the little one, we made a cross for you, and we pounded it into the snow, and it stood up nice and tall. Do you like it, Lord? We had lots of good things to eat, but Doug said we had to be careful just in case we got lost or sump'n.

Everything was exciting and fun, but coming down the mountain I couldn't jump as far as Dougie, 'cause he's over six feet tall and has really long legs. I ended up in water up to my knees, and it was s-o-o-o-o cold! My brother really loves me, but when he gets angry, he talks through his teeth just like Mom. Must be 'cause they're related, huh? Anyway, he built a fire and dried my socks, but it was beginning to get dark, and we had a long way to go to get home. A search party was all ready to go up and find us, 'cause there are wild pigs in these mountains. We could hear them sometimes. We walked out just in time, and Mom and Daddy were really happy to see us.

We prayed a lot, and I thank you so much for helping us find the right way out, Lord. Daddy and Mom weren't even angry that I got my snow pants wet. That was strange. Thanks again, Lord, I sure do love you!

GETTIN' OUR CHRISTMAS TREE

Today was a very strange day. I don't know if I will ever understand grown-ups, Lord! Today is the day we get our Christmas tree; it should be a fun time, right? WRONG! My grandfather, Gar, almost always brings us a Christmas tree, and my Mom and Daddy never like it, but they don't say anything until Gar leaves. My mother starts talking through her teeth again; it seems to me she says the same thing every year, something about screaming!

Gar seems to look for the loneliest tree he can find, one with hardly any branches. Maybe he feels sorry for the skinny ones, or maybe 'cause they're so ugly he likes to get rid of 'em. He always says the same thing, "A tree's a tree, and you'll never know the difference when it's trimmed."

Well this year, I guess Mom and Daddy both figured the tree was hopeless, so we all went out to find another tree. We found some beauties. We cut the top off one, but it was so big and heavy we couldn't carry it out. We got it partway though, and Daddy said, "Oh, I've strained myself. We'll have to leave it and use the one Gar brought us." On the way out of the woods, we all stepped in a bog and had water up to our knees, and our boots made that funny sound when we walked, slop, slop, slop! Daddy started talking through his teeth, that's only the second time I ever heard Daddy do that. I do hope it's not catching.

When Gar came down the next day, Daddy and Mom told Gar that was the prettiest tree he'd ever gotten them. Tell me, Lord; is it a sin to lie?

Thank you for making trees for us to decorate. I'm just not sure why we decorate trees to celebrate your birthday. Maybe when I get older I'll understand, but you could tell me now if you want to, Lord. I like to celebrate your birthday, Jesus, because you were born to die to take my sins. My Sunday school teacher told me all about you. I'm sure glad I asked you to be my Savior. I can't think of anything to give you for a present, Lord, just my love. Is that good enough?

Tell me, Lord, does it seem to you people forget what Christmas is all about? Some people look sad at Christmastime. Daddy says, it's because they're running out of money, but it's your birthday. Do they give you money, Lord? I don't think you care much about money. I'll give you my heart, Jesus. You'll have to help me though. I try so hard to do what's right, but sometimes I do wrong. Tell me, Lord, why do you love me so much?

TROUBLE IN THE SCHOOLYARD

Today was the worst day of my whole life, Lord! Here I was with Joan, my best friend. We were just trying to do something simple like break a long piece of licorice, like we always do with our teeth.

Dumb ol' Asa Greeneau ran right through that piece of licorice strung from Joan's mouth to mine, and I couldn't believe it! My two front teeth came right out of my mouth! I got blood all over my new dress, and Asa laughed, and then when the teacher was cleaning me up, she laughed too. I've never been so humiliated in my whole life.

The teacher sent me home from school, and I heard her whisper to another teacher sump'n' about "Grandma Moses," whoever that is. I decided on the way home that when I told Mom and Daddy about it they would beat Asa up, but Lord, do you know what they did? They looked at me and laughed. Only Judy gave me a hug. They tried to pretend they weren't laughing, but I could see their eyes laughing right at me, and I don't think that was very nice at all. Did you laugh at me too, Lord? I don't think so.

I found a piece of chalk, and I went up and down the whole sidewalk, and I wrote "I hate Asa Greeneau," and I felt better for a little while, but now I don't feel so good. I know I'm not supposed to hate, Lord, but how would you feel if somebody knocked your two front teeth out? I guess you know just how I felt, 'cause my Sunday school teacher said you were beaten up really bad before they tried to kill you...but they couldn't kill you, no matter how hard they tried, huh, Lord!

When I looked in the mirror, I was surprised; I will never smile again until my teeth grow in! I am so ugly lookin', Lord, even Judy laughed at me when I came downstairs. I really do hate Asa, Lord. Now I know I'm not supposed to hate, but I'd like to knock his two front teeth out and see how he liked it! I feel like my Mom, Lord...I'd talk through my teeth right now, if I had any and ask you for strength too. Help me to forgive Asa, Lord; it'll be awful hard for me, but if you help me a whole lot, just maybe I can...but it doesn't mean I'll love Asa, either.

OH NO! MUMPS!

I thought yesterday was the worst day of my life; well, I've got news for you, Lord. It wasn't. Today is! I started to get ready for school, and it hurt to brush my teeth, the ones I had left, that is, and it hurt to open my mouth to eat breakfast. Phooey, I didn't want to go to school today anyway with no front teeth.

Mom looked at me kinda funny, and she went and got a sweet pickle and made me eat it for breakfast. Can you imagine that? I spit it out real fast, it tasted so sour! Mom said I had the mumps, and I had to stay home, and all of a sudden my cheeks started getting all swollen up.. When I looked in the mirror, I was one sad lookin' person, and then I started cryin'!

Dougie came home from school and we sat down for supper. He looked at me and said I looked just like a jack-o'-lantern and fell right off his chair laughing at me. Lord, am I gonna have to spend the rest of my life with people laughing at me? Judy didn't laugh at me; she just hugged me real tight!

Two people love me beside you, Lord. Good ol' Dr. Bates said to me, "Well, dear, you've got the mumps on both sides, you poor little dear, but you're still my beautiful little girl, and you'll be good as new in about ten days!" You, Judy, and Dr. Bates are the only ones in the whole world who didn't laugh at me. Thank you, Judy, Dr. Bates, and Jesus.

I'm trying real hard not to smile around the house, but it's awful hard, Lord. Daddy says he misses my smile, and he promised he wouldn't laugh at me anymore, if I would just be me and smile again. I really haven't felt very good today, Lord, but I always feel better when Mom rocks me in the big wicker rocking chair. I'm kinda big to be rocked, but Mom said it was okay when you're not feeling good to be rocked. and she said she was sorry she laughed at me too, and you know what, Lord? I couldn't help it, a great big smile sneaked out, and I feel a whole lot better now. Thank you for not laughing at me, Lord. I won't say I hate Asa anymore, Lord, but I don't love him, either.

FUN AT THE LAKE

Today has been, as my Aunt Winnie says, "a supamellagorgeous day." School is finished, and we've got the whole summer ahead of us. We're all at the little camp on Sapontic Lake we share with Gar and Nannie. We've got it all to ourselves for ten whole days. Boy, are we gonna have fun!

Mom brought along a girl to help take care of us kids so she and Daddy can have fun too. I think maybe Daddy doesn't like having this girl along with us. He got awful mad this mornin', Lord!

This girl, Shirley, was acting all put out 'cause Mom and Daddy went fishin' yesterday and left us all behind. Mom felt sorry for her, so she took Shirley out fishin' early this morning. Well, Lord, did you see what happened? Judy got up right after Mom and Shirley left and used the pot, 'cause we don't have an inside toilet at camp; BUT, she left it open right in front of Daddy's bed. When Daddy got up, he stepped right in the pot and turned it over, and poor Daddy. First his face turned red, and he started huffin' and puffin' like he always does when he gets mad, and he was roaring for Mom! Tell me, Lord, is this what is known as a rage? If it is, he had one! He cleaned the mess up, and in between huffs and puffs, yelled out the door for Mom to get home. Poor Judy didn't know what she had done wrong.

Daddy finally started breakfast for us kids, and Dougie and I are sitting there with our shoulders just a-shakin' 'cause we were laughin' so hard and trying not to make any noise. Finally I couldn't hold it any longer, and then Dougie burst out too, and Daddy stood with his eyes just glarin' at us, like he was the devil or sump'n'' and began talkin' through his teeth! About that time, in walked Mom with Shirley; and Daddy was still talkin' through his teeth like Mom and Dougie do. I'm glad I don't, Lord. Mom started laughin', and pretty soon I saw a smile start in Daddy's eyes, and he sat down and laughed and laughed while he was tellin' Mom the story of Judy and the pot.

Are all parents like this, Lord? Are you sure you sent me to the right ones?

BEAR AND RACCOONS

This sure is an exciting vacation, Lord! Last night we had a bear pawin' at the window right next to Mom and Daddy's bed. Mom woke up 'cause the window is on her side of the bed, and she looked that bear right in the face. Well, sir, we all woke up when we heard Mom scream, and all Mom could do was point at the empty window. Now how were we supposed to know there was a bear at the window just a second before?

We had just gotten settled down to sleep again, when we heard Spotty, our dog, howlin' and cryin' and carryin' on something fierce! Everybody jumped up again, and Dad looked out on the porch, and there were about five raccoons tryin' to get our potatoes. The raccoons were clawing Spotty, jumpin' on him, and everythin'. Poor Spotty was howling and bleedin', so my Dad went out to rescue him.

Lord, you've seen my Daddy in his funny-lookin' ski pajamas; well, out he goes in those. He started pushing at the raccoons to get them off

Spotty, but they just turned on him and swatted him all over. Daddy yelled at Mom to get him a stick to hit them with, and poor Mom, when she gets in a tight fix, Daddy says, "Her mind does not work too well."

Mom grabbed a little tiny twig about six inches long and handed it out the door to Daddy, who bellowed again just like he did when he stepped in the pot. He started talkin' through his teeth again and asking you to help him Lord. I guess his yellin' must have scared the raccoons off, because they left right away, or maybe you just had pity on Daddy and made 'em leave.

Mom fixed a big pot of coffee and made us kids some coffee-milk, and we all talked about what we would do the next time the same thing happened, and we all ended up laughin' about it, even Daddy. Lord, did you see Daddy with that little twig in his hand? Wasn't he funny lookin', Lord? Thanks for takin' care of the raccoons, Lord, and not lettin' my Daddy and Spotty get hurt. I love you, Lord!

LIVER AND ONIONS

Mom is a really good cook, and I like everythin' she makes most of the time, but my brother Dougie doesn't like a lot of things.

Mom made liver and onions for supper tonight, and Dougie started in makin' a fuss, telling me it would make me sick, just like it does him.

I took a taste and immediately got sick right there at the table. Mom got me all cleaned up, and Daddy sent Dougie away from the table and told me to sit down.

Daddy told me, "Just because Dougie doesn't like liver and onions doesn't mean it's not good. I want you to forget what he said and try and taste it again. You are just like me, Lila Jane, and I think you will like it."

I had to think about it for a few minutes, but Mom always told us to try something before you say you don't like it. It isn't much fun to eat after you've been sick, Lord, but I decided if Daddy liked, it, I probably would too. So I squeezed my eyes shut and took a great big bite of that liver, and guess what. It tasted good, and I ate the whole thing. Dougie was wrong; liver and onions taste good!

GRAMMY AND PAPA'S TABLE

We used to go out and visit Grammy and Papa almost every Sunday after church. It was a lot of fun.

Mom used to do a whole bunch of cookin', 'cause Grammy had a lot of shocks, they called them, and she couldn't walk good or do any cookin' anymore.

We used to gather 'round this big ol' oak table, and there were aunts and uncles and cousins there every Sunday. Lots of food was on the table, especially in the summer when Papa had his garden. Sometimes we just had all fresh vegetables, and it was really good.

There was so much talkin' though, it was hard to hear what anybody was sayin'. Grammy would try and try to say something, but her voice wasn't very strong usually, and all of a sudden I would hear, "MY GOOSE!" Everything got very quiet and Grammy would say what she wanted to say, and when she was finished, off we'd all go again.

Papa was a wonderful grandfather, he did funny

things, like he could eat his peas with a knife, and when he drank his coffee or tea, he poured it in his saucer. Never saw that before, did you, Lord?

After we ate, Papa would always sing a little ditty for us kids. He never forgot the words, either. One of 'em he used to sing was about takin' his girl to the pitcher show and takin' her out for sump'n' to eat afterward. "She said she wasn't hungry, and this is what she ett." Then he would go on and on and on about what she ett, but he had but fifteen cents. Papa always said "ett"; he never said "ate" like we were told.

Once when we were on our way out to their house, Mom had a made a beautiful cake and was holding it in her lap, when all of a sudden a car swerved right near us. Well, now, that cake went a-flyin'. Mom started cryin' about the cake, and Dad started huffin' and puffin' again, like he does when he's upset.

We just slid into the snow bank, so there was nothin' wrong with the car, but Dad was really up-set because Mom was more upset over the cake than she was the car.

It's a good thing you were there protectin' us, Lord. Parents are very strange sometimes, Lord!

GRAMMY'S CELLAR!

One of the most scary, but interestin', things to do when I was with Grammy and Papa was when they asked me to get something way down in the cellar.

Grammy used to can lots of food during harvest time. I could find strawberry, raspberry, and blueberry jam and jellies; apple butter; and lots of fresh apples, all different kinds.

Every vegetable Papa raised was canned, except potatoes were kept raw, 'cause it was cool down there. Papa told me that's why they could keep things from summer, right through to spring. People don't do that much anymore, do they, Lord. I wonder why.

My Uncle Donnie used to love to scare me down there. The cellar was big, and it had lots of shadows, and he would go down before me and jump out at me and really scare me, but then we laughed.

Grammy and Papa didn't have a toilet that flushed; they had a "two-holer" connected to the barn. Donnie painted it blue with yellow notes on it, and it said, "I've got the back-house blues!"

I used to love to feed the cows and watch Papa separate and strain the milk. That was fun. He'd squirt milk to the cats, and they loved it.

GRAMMY AND PAPA'S FAMILY

Grammy and Papa had eleven children, so the house was never empty, and when all the families got together, we had a great time.

Papa used to chew tobacco. I will never forget that, and he had an old can near the back of the pot-belly stove that he used to spit in. He never missed that can. It made a big tinny sound every time he spit, and Grammy would always say, "Morey, stop that!"

There was a big ol' piano in Grammy's room, and we would all gather 'round that and sing and sing and sing, with Mom playing.

All of us kids had a chance to either act out something or sing, and it was like being on the stage, with everybody clapping.

Uncle Clayton could make a regular ol' saw sound really pretty. I don't know how he did it, but it sure was pretty.

Grammy and Papa had a big house with two stoves; one in the living room with a hole in the ceiling where they kept the wood for the pot-belly stove, and a cook stove in the kitchen. When we woke up we would run down into the kitchen where it was nice and warm. Nobody complained about anythin' either, Lord. That stove had a place where the water got hot on the end of the stove, cause there wasn't any hot water faucet, but nobody cared.

Papa says we're all spoiled now. Maybe we are, Lord!

We used to swim out to the islands, and it was a long way out, but I was a good swimmer. Poor Mom, whenever she saw me out in the middle of the lake she screamed at me, and I just pretended I couldn't hear her. 'course you can hear everything on the lake. She always sent Dougie out to get me, but he never learned. I always rocked the boat when he was reaching for me, and I pulled him in! I laughed and laughed, and he did too ...after a while!

It was fun staying at Grammy and Papa's. Right next door they had a one-room schoolhouse, and boy, that teacher was good. Those kids learned really fast, 'cause you heard all the lessons from each class, if you were listening.

We saw calves, colts, and kittens being born, and chicks cracking through their shells; got chased by the rooster and goose, and that was fun, Lord! Papa had one cow that learned to lift the fence post with her horns, and she would let all the other cows out. We would have to go all over town getting them and making sure they stayed out of the road and out of gardens. That one cow was really smart, and she was hard to catch. About the only way we could catch her was when there was a car comin' and she got scared. That's when she'd let me get her. Papa said that she gave the best milk.

NANNIE'S SHEETS

Nannie gets up early on Monday mornings and does her wash. She gets up really early, even before I get up.

We have a good time together on washday, though. My other grandfather, Gar, helps her pour really hot water in these big ol' tubs, and she swishes all the sheets around with a wooden paddle.

I don't know why it was so important to Gar, but Nannie had to get her sheets out before anybody else in the neighborhood. She used to work hard getting those sheets nice and white; she used so much bleach it made my eyes water. So did hers, but Gar's never watered. After she washed and rinsed the sheets I don't know how many times, she put blue stuff in the water, and then they really came out white.

Nannie was awful tired after doin' the wash, I wanna tell ya, I got tired just watchin' her. When she was finished, she'd hang 'em out on the clothes-line, and Gar would look very proud.

Nannie and I would have some of her wonderful

chocolate donuts and a big glass of milk together, and we talked for a long time.

Gar walked all around the neighborhood to see who had their wash out by six A.M. and would inspect all the washed clothes and come back and tell Nannie that hers were the whitest of all of them. I don't think Nannie really cared that much; she just wanted clean sheets.

THE FOURTH OF JULY

We always celebrated the Fourth of July at Gar and Nannie's, and Gar always got lots of firecrackers to set off.

Gar smoked a cigar. I like the smell of cigars, do you, Lord? He would give us his cigar to light the firecrackers with, and always told us to run real fast after we got the end lit. We did, but Dougie and I always tried to sneak a puff off that ol' cigar.

Every time I took a puff, it made me feel sick, and Gar always had a funny grin on his face, just waitin' for Dougie and me to get sick. Our faces felt like they turned green, but after a while the bad feelin' went away, but after that, I never took a puff off that nasty cigar again.

Gar put firecrackers in cans, and they made a big noise and blew the can way far in the air. Mom and Daddy didn't like us to play with firecrackers, but it's nice to have grandparents; they let us do things Mom and Daddy would never let us do.

SINGIN' IN THE RAIN

Do you like jumpin' in puddles, Lord? That's one of my favorite things to do, course ya get pretty wet when ya do it, but it's so much fun.

Whenever it rains, Patty and Peta, the twins, and I swing around and dance like we saw in the pitcha show once. Sometimes we even use an umbrella.

The last time Peta danced around, she poked Patty in the head with the end of her umbrella, and her mother was wicked mad at her, but we still do it over near my house.

Peta and I have yellow raincoats, but Patty has a blue one, I guess so they don't get them mixed up, 'cause they are twins. They don't look alike at all though, Lord. Peta is a little chubby like me, and Patty is kinda skinny and doesn't like to get dirty.

We have lotsa fun together most of the time, and it sure is good to have friends!

OLD FRIENDS AT THE WHARF

Ya know, Lord, sometimes I don't understand mothers. I'm a big girl now. I'm almost eight years old, and Mom still treats me like I'm a baby.

Sometimes I get tired of watchin' Judy, so when Mom ties Judy out so she won't run into the road, I go down to the wharf and talk with all the old fellas. They sit on the edge of the wharf for hours just talkin' and jokin'. They like me to sit and tell them what's goin' on at my house, and then they laugh!

Where we live, the water comes up really high, and Mom gets real nervous when I sit with these old friends, 'cause she's afraid I'm gonna fall in. They would never let me fall in the water, though. They always watch me and tell me when I need to sit back and all that stuff.

Besides that, I've got a dog named Spotty, and he follows me wherever I go, so I wish you would make Mom not worry so much about me.

Sometimes I can see the big fish come in to eat the little fish when I'm sittin' on the wharf. I went up to get my fishin' rod one day, but my old friends wouldn't let me use it. They said, "The fish will pull you right into the water with your little fishin' pole." I guess probably they're right.

One day one of my old friends brought me his fishin' rod and held on tight to me when I caught a pretty big fish. We all ate that fish for supper that night. I was really proud. Daddy works hard to make money so we can have good food 'n' stuff, so maybe I can catch some more, if Mom would leave me alone and let me do it!

You wouldn't let me fall off the wharf anyway, would you, Lord?

PLAYIN' IN THE DITCH

I've got a friend named Ronnie. We have a good time together playing in the water that runs down the ditch by the side of the road.

We make little boats and stuff, and we can start them way up at the other end of the road, and they come floatin' down just great! We've tried makin' boats out of lots of different things. Tree bark works really good.

Ronnie and I have played many times in the ditch. It isn't stinky water or anything. I don't know where it comes from, though, and neither does Ronnie. One day Ronnie wasn't at school, and when I went to his house, nobody was there; they were all away at a big hospital.

When they finally came home, Ronnie couldn't walk very good. He got polio. They said it was from playin' in the water…but how come I didn't get sick, Lord? Ronnie doesn't act very happy, and he has somethin' on his leg to help him walk better.

When Mom found out, she was talkin' through her teeth again, Lord, and she hugged me so tight I could hardly breathe. She really confuses me, Lord. One minute she's talkin' through her teeth, which usually means I've done somethin' wrong, and the next minute she's huggin' me. Mom had Dr. Bates talk to me, and he told me, "Never play in that ditch water again."

EATIN' AT MY FRIEND'S HOUSE

I have a nice friend, and her mom likes her to eat dried prunes, so she gives me some too. We sit on her porch steps in the sun and watch the seagulls try to get some of our prunes, but we don't give 'em any.

Do you eat prunes, Lord? They make me go to the bathroom a lot, so I don't eat too many of them. I like my friend very much, and I really like her mother, but her father is very strange.

I was invited to eat supper with them once, and at dinnertime in our house we talk about everything that happened during the day. Well, sir, I sat down, and everything was eerie quiet. Nobody said anythin'.

I looked around, and everybody was lookin' down at their plates. Nobody was lookin' at each other, and nobody said a word. I said, "What is wrong with you people?"

The father said, "We do not speak at mealtimes."

Mom says I did "THE UNSPEAKABLE," whatever that is: I excused myself and left. I will never eat there again! What a way to live. I'm sure if I had taken a bite, it would have stuck in my throat and I'd have gotten sick, so it's a good thing I came home.

All Daddy said was, "He's a strange one, all right!" Well, I guess so! Do you talk at the table, Lord? I betcha do. We're gonna have a big banquet up there with you someday when we get to live with you, that's what my Sunday school teacher said.

THE NAVY LANDED

W e have a whole bunch of Seabees that landed; everywhere I look I see them.

Mom and Dad go over and play the piano and saxophone for them, and they dance and dance and dance. All the local women come to dance with them and make them happy before they ship out to war.

Mom and Dad take me along and set me on top of the piano and have me sing. Sometimes the men come over, touch my hair, or give me a hug 'cause "They miss their own kids so much," Dad says.

Sometimes I see them crying when I sing, "I'm a Little on the Lonely Side" or "My Buddy." I guess it's 'cause they are so lonely.

Mom and Dad have one special man who comes to our house a lot. His name is Arnold. He's Spanish and taught Mom how to Roombah or sump'n' like that. He likes us kids and gives us chocolate bars and stuff we can't get right now 'cause of the war.

Daddy is a part of the National Guard. His eyes

aren't good enough to join the military, they told him. He was very disappointed. He is a warden, and when we have blackouts, he goes around and makes sure all our lights are off. I got a little lantern that has different colors in it, and he caught me in my window with it lighted. He was very upset with me. I wonder if my Bambi pictures that light up in the dark show up too. I sure hope not!

It was a very sad day for all of us when Arnold left. We all cried really hard. He said he would come back to see us and bring his wife and children. I sure hope he does. He went to Okinawa, some-place far, far away.

We heard from him two times, and at Christ-mastime, he sent us a whole great big box of chocolate bars. Wow! We shared them with lots of people, Daddy said, "That was the right thing to do."

We didn't hear from Arnold again. I hope he didn't get killed, but if he did, he's with you, Lord. We just continue to pray for him and his family, though.

FOOLIN' MOM

It's gettin' nice and warm now, Lord, and the park has a nice new swimming pool. They give free swimming lessons too, and I'm takin' 'em. So are the twins and my big brother, Doug.

Mom says we can go swimmin' as long as the thermometer says it's seventy degrees or more. Well, now, it's been a little bit chilly, so Dougie and I take turns showin' Mom the thermometer outside.

We finally figured out a way to get it up to seventy degrees. If one of us goes out and puts our hands on it for a few minutes it will go right up to where we need it. We take turns getting Mom to see the thermometer, then we scooch way down so she can't see us when she's lookin' at the thermometer. It works every time. Is that cheatin', Lord? The water's always warm once you get in, anyway.

MY BROTHER DOESN'T LOVE ME!

You know I love my brother Dougie very much. In fact, when I wake up too early, he lets me come and get in bed with him, so I don't get yelled at.

I've climbed in bed with Dougie as long as I can remember, and then guess what happened, Lord. I crawled into bed with him, and he pushed me right out of his bed and said I'm not allowed to get in his bed anymore.

I cried and woke everybody up. Mom made me get back in my own bed. I got back in, but I didn't go to sleep, so there!

Daddy said that now that Dougie was older, I had to stay in my own bed or room until everybody got up. He said Dougie was matoorin', whatever that is.

Come to think of it, he's been actin' kinda strange lately; spends a lot of time in the bathroom slickin' down his hair. I watched him once. He put spit on his finger and tried to get this little wavy thing to stand up on the top of his hair. Does that mean he's interested in girls now? Hmm…maybe that's what this is all about.

I betcha I'm right! There's some kind of a class ball comin' up, and Dougie had to invite a GIRL to march in with. I guess they're getting all gussied up for it. He chose Joanne Baldasarro; she's a real pretty Italian girl who lives up the street. Mom's got 'em both in there teachin' them how to dance. Dougie stepped on her toes FIVE TIMES; I counted. She didn't cry or yell or anything. She fluttered her big brown eyes at him, and he turned all red. Is this what love is all about? It's kinda silly, if ya ask me.

SCARLET FEVER

I got really sick the other night, as you know, Lord. I woke up, and I was so hot I could hardly breathe.

I called to Mom and Daddy, and they had to rush me to the hospital, my fever was so high. My good ol' Dr. Bates wasn't there, so I had another doctor, but I was so sick I didn't care.

The doctor said I had scarlet fever. I had a big rash all over me. They put me in a private room and wouldn't let anybody in or out. It was like bein' put in jail...at least that's what I think it must be like.

Doctors and nurses came in with those white things over their mouths and special gloves and everything. They kept giving me shots of pennysillin or sump'n' like that and it just made me worse and worse. I had bumps all over my body, Lord; you saw me, and the sheets they use in there weren't soft like Mom's and Nannie's...they were stiff and made my bumps and rash even worse.

I begged Mom and Daddy to take me home, but

the doctor said "No," and I had to stay! Finally they realized I was allergic to that pennycillin stuff they were givin' me. After about ten days I got to go home…FINALLY!

Where was good old Dr. Bates when I needed him? I don't like going to doctors or hospitals, Lord, do you?

Anyway, now I'm home, and nobody else in the family got scarlet fever, so that's a good thing. Have you had scarlet fever, Lord?

I DROVE DAD'S CAR

Boy, oh boy, did I get in trouble today! Dad lets me steer the car when I'm in his lap, and he tells me I was doin' really good, so...I decided to try drivin' myself.

He had showed me how to make the car go back and forward, so I did it and went backward, right across the street into somebody else's yard. I didn't hit anything, but did you hear Dougie and Dad and Mom screaming their heads off? I bet the whole world could hear them. The whole neighborhood heard them and came out and looked to see what was goin' on. They were all gawkin' at me. I felt like sayin' the same thing Mom does with her mouth, askin' you for strength, but I didn't do it.

Dad ran over and pulled the keys out of the car so I stopped goin' backward and told me never, ever to do that again. He told me it was a good thing you were lookin' out for me, 'cause they didn't have eyes in the back of their heads to see what I would do next. I don't think that was a very nice thing to say to me.

Dr. Bates was drivin' by and he stopped, and do you know what Mom asked him? She asked him if there was a pill they could give me to make me quiet, and good ol' Dr. Bates said, "Not a thing to do; she's got extra energy, called hypa-active, and she'll always be the same." I just hope they don't try to tie me out like they do Judy!

Daddy said that I couldn't drive until I was all grown up. I just wonder why he showed me how to drive, if he didn't want me to drive! Grownups are strange, Lord, don' cha think so? I told Dad I was sorry though for makin' him worry.

PAPA'S AMAZING MACHINE

I like to go out to the barn with Papa when he milks the cows; it's a lot of fun. Ya know Papa's cows are all just a little bit different, just like people; that's what I think, anyway.

We've got Dorry, who can pick up the fence post with her horns and let all the other cows out. Susie, who is kinda shy until she gets to know ya, and then there is Bossy. She likes to kick the bucket over when Papa's milkin' her. She will kick at you, too, if you're not careful.

Papa says that you made cows different, just like you made people different. I guess that's a good thing. Papa says it's a really good thing you made us all just a little bit different. Come to think of it, Mom keeps telling you she's glad you made only one of me. I can't figure that out, Lord. Do you think maybe she doesn't love me very much? Sometimes I think she loves Judy more than she loves me, but Papa said, she just has to give Judy more attention because she has special needs.

I like to feed the cows. They have great big

tongues, and sometimes they lick my hand by mistake when I'm feeding 'em.

Papa gives every cat and kitten a little squirt of milk when he's milkin', and they really like that!

After Papa's milkin' is over, we carry the buckets in to put the milk in Papa's amazing machine. First he puts cheesecloth over the top of the machine. He says it keeps out anything that doesn't belong in the milk. He has a handle he turns, and all of a sudden the cream comes out one spout, and the milk comes out the other. I don't understand how that machine knows which is the cream and which is the milk. Do you understand that, Lord? It is my Papa's amazing machine; he said so!

After we separate the cream and milk, we put it in bottles that are boiled on the stove, to make sure there's no contampanashun or sump'n' like that. I really like cream. Papa likes plain ol' milk, and Grammy likes buttermilk. Mom doesn't like milk at all. I can't understand that, Lord!

MOM AND THE FISH

Sometimes when Daddy is watching Judy, Mom and I go down to the lakeshore, all by ourselves. We have a good time talkin' about what we're gonna do that day.

Mom told me today she was very proud of the way I help her take care of Judy. I asked Mom why Judy is "special." Judy was a real pretty baby, she said, and she was a good baby, but once when Mom was so tired out and had to do some shopping, she had a woman come in and watch us kids. She found out that the older lady was givin' Judy a bath, like she told her not to do, because soapy babies are really slippy-slidey, the woman dropped her and caused brain damage. After she was dropped, her eyes crossed, and there was nothing anybody could do, not even Dr. Bates. Judy has to be watched all the time, and that is Dougie's and my job when Mom is busy.

While we were at the shore today, Mom saw a great big fish floatin' on top of the water. Mom was really excited. We ran back to camp, and she brought it in and showed Dad, and he looked at her with a great big twinkle in his eyes and laughed so hard tears ran down his face.

Well, Lord, Mom and I thought he'd be real happy, but he laughed hard, and finally he said, "Arlene, that is a sucker; you can't eat suckers!"

Mom and I were real disappointed, so we went back down and went fishin' and caught three bass and two pickerel, so I guess we showed Dad! It was fun to be with Mom all by myself.

GRAMMY'S COOKIE JAR

My Grammy has a pantry where she keeps all of her cookin' and stuff, and she makes some of the best cookies anybody in the whole world could make.

Dougie and I used to go in and sneak cookies and take 'em down to the shore and sit and watch the waves come in. We didn't think Grammy knew we were snitchin' those cookies.

We came up from the shore, and there was Grammy bakin' some more cookies, and Dougie looked all guilty and everything and I asked Grammy what she was makin'.

Grammy looked at me with her big brown eyes and said, "Well, dear, since you and Dougie have eaten most of the cookies, I will have to make some more."

Oh boy....wait 'til Mom and Daddy find out! Grammy said, "I've known all along that you were getting into the cookie jar, and you know...all you had to do was ask for cookies, and you could have had them. You didn't have to sneak them."

We both started cryin' 'cause we had sneaked those cookies, but Grammy told us, "Stop crying; no real harm done, but ask the next time." She didn't tell Mom and Daddy, either, but Dougie and I both agreed we would never take cookies without askin' anymore.

Sure am glad we didn't get into trouble with Mom and Daddy, but I think maybe we got in trouble with you, Lord, 'cause you saw us all the time, didn't you? Just like Grammy knew all the time; Papa knew, too, and he told us afterward "That's how thieves start. First they steal little things like cookies and candy, but then it goes on to money and tobacco and stuff."

I won't take things anymore, Lord, unless I ask. I guess Dougie and I are kinda glad we got caught. We don't want to become thieves, Lord.

JUDY GOT RUN OVER

This has been a very excitin' day, Lord, but not a good day for our Judy. Ya know we call her "Judy-bug." I'm not sure why we do that, but we do.

Judy loves to run, but because her eyes are crossed, sometimes she runs right into things. That's why Dougie and Mom and I have to help watch her really carefully.

Judy-bug just got out of our sight, and when Daddy drove in the yard, Judy-bug ran out to meet him, fell down, and got her arm run over. She was cryin', Mom was cryin', Daddy had tears in his eyes, and Dougie and I didn't know what to do.

Judy-bug's arm was all bloody and looked terrible. Mom called Dr. Bates, but he was away, so we went to this other doctor in town. He said she needed stitches, and stitched her up.

We all told Judy-bug she must never do that again, but we don't know if she really understood, but she sure got scared of the car, anyway.

Well, everything was goin' okay for about three

days, when Judy-bug's arm began looking terrible. Her arm was all filled with pus, and it smelled bad, too. We all went to see Dr. Bates and he took one look at it and said something like, "Who in the name of God did this?"

Mom told him what happened, and he had to give Judy-bug a shot to keep her from hurtin', and he cleaned all the gravel and dirt out of where she got run over.

Dr. Bates gave Judy-bug a big hug and kiss and gave each one of us a really good lollipop. We love Dr. Bates. I bet you love Dr. Bates too. He always tells us that you are the really the one who heals; he only follows your orders, Lord. I think Dr. Bates loves you almost as much as I love you.

Judy-bug's arm is healing up really good now, Lord. Thank you for helping Dr. Bates get all that stuff cleaned out, and thank you for healing it up real quick.

BOYDEN'S LAKE

Here we are in Perry, Maine, Lord, waitin' to find a house in Eastport to live in. Daddy got transferred here, so because it's summertime, we are renting a camp on Boyden's Lake for a while.

Boyden's Lake is a nice lake, but lots of people get drowned in this lake. I'm not sure just why that is, but it happens.

Dougie and Mom and I went out fishin', and we were catching lots of fish, just having a great time, when all of a sudden a bad wind came up and started makin' the boat sway back and forth, and water started comin' in.

My brother is good at just about everything around the lake. He's good with startin' boat motors and everything! He tried startin' the motor, but water kept washing over the motor, and he tried and tried, and finally he got it started. We made for home, and all the way, the water splashed in the boat. Mom and I got on the bottom of the boat, all scrunched down. Dougie said, "Start praying!"

Mom said, "Honey, I've been praying since the wind first started!"

You know I was prayin', Lord. First I prayed the motor would start, and then I just started thankin' you for getting us home...and you did!

Daddy and Judy-bug were right there at the shore waitin' for us to get in. Daddy says he thinks Boyden's Lake is just a very dangerous lake. The winds come up quicker than Papa's lake, and there are no islands to run to.

Do you think some people pray only when they're in trouble, Lord? Is that a fair thing to do? You've told me so many times, when I start to get upset when things are goin' wrong, to thank you for bringin' me through bad times. It works, Lord!

SKUNKS AND PIES!

Gar and Nannie came over to stay at the camp on Boyden's Lake with us, so Dougie and I got to sleep in the tent.

Dougie's a Boy Scout, so he knows how to put up tents really good, and he likes sleepin' in a tent. I'm not so sure about sleepin' in the tent, 'cause it has a few holes in it, and it smells kinda funny; but cha have to do what cha hafta do, Daddy says.

Mom always makes lots of pies and cakes and good stuff for us, whether we have company or not. At camp here, there's only an ice box, so there's not much room for the stuff she makes, but Daddy built a wooden box outside for her to put her pies she made 'specially for Gar and Nannie comin'.

Gar and Mom don't seem to get along very well. I'm not sure why, but they just don't. I think Gar likes everythin' perfect, but ya know, Lord, everythin' is not always perfect. I think sometimes Judy-bug makes him nervous, 'cause she runs into stuff so much. Now we know Judy-bug is special, and we love her just the way she is. Mom seems to say

"God give me strength" a lot more when Gar is around. I've noticed that. Have you?

We were sleepin' in the tent when we heard a growl, and we have bears around the lake, so we stayed real quiet. We peeked out the tent flap, and that bear was tryin' to get into Mom's pies in the box Dad built for her. Well sir, as if that wasn't bad enough, there was a skunk there too. The skunk sprayed the bear and the box, 'cause the skunk was tryin' to get the pies too.

That bear took off runnin' right into the woods, just a rubbin' his eyes. The skunk was still tryin' to get into the pies until Daddy turned the light on, and it went away. It smelled sump'n' awful. I just wonder why you made skunks.

That afternoon it was time to eat dinner together before Gar and Nannie left to go home. Mom served a nice dinner, and then went to get the pies. Oh, dear, Lord; those pies smelled terrible, I was not going to take one bite, no siree-bob! Daddy took a bite; Mom took a bite; Nannie took a bite; Dougie and Judy, too. and they all put their forks down. because it smelled and tasted like skunk spray. Now Gar…he sat there and ate his whole piece of pie, and he told the rest of us, "There's nothin' wrong with this pie!"

Mom says Gar is the most stubborn man she has ever known, and I guess she's right, Lord. Why do you suppose Gar ate that terrible smellin' and tastin' pie? Did you laugh? I betcha did!

LILA JANE TIBBITTS

Lila Jane is cofounder-and vice president of Bridge Ministries Inc. based in Titusville, Florida, in the United States.

She and her husband, Frank, have been missionary/evangelists for more than forty years, ministering throughout the United States, the United Kingdom, Canada, Bahamas, Philippines, Ghana, Togo, Nigeria, Liberia, Tanzania, India and Pakistan. They are church planters, having established churches in all of these countries as well as founding an ACE School and a Feeding Program for 200 children in the Philippines.

BMI is registered as a nonprofit corporation in the United States with 501 (c) (3) status, bringing Bridge Ministries Inc. under the Full Gospel Ministerial and Church Fellowship in Texas, and it is also registered with the SEC in Ghana, Togo, and the Philippines and as a nonprofit charity in Canada, registered with Revenue Canada.

Currently Lila Jane is the assistant pastor with the Bridge of Love Fellowship in Titusville, Florida. She and her husband minister to ex-drug addicts and ex-alcoholics and have a wonderful group of steadfast Christians who help support their efforts. People are coming to the, Lord, which is their goal.

Lila Jane was named Outstanding Young Woman of Maine in 1971, while her husband served in Vietnam. In England she was also named Outstanding United States Air Force Security Service Wife of the Year in 1972. In 2004, she was the Featured Poet in *The International Who's Who in Poetry*. It is very kind to be recognized by these various groups, but Lila Jane says, "The most important 'happening' in my life is knowing Jesus Christ as my Savior and the fact that He knows me better than I know myself and still loves me!"

There is a definite anointing on Lila Jane's writings and ministry. She has the ability to take everyday events and make people laugh with her, while bringing the happenings into a Christian perspective. Today, my friends, we need something to laugh about, so enjoy this book, and perhaps it will bring back some of your own comical incidents.

Printed in the United States
203140BV00002B/13-60/P

9 781432 718817